Thank you to my parents for allowing my green blankie to be part
of my childhood and all my adventures.

To my kiddos, Evan, Wyatt and Lucy, thank you for bringing lovey adventures to life!
Without you as my inspiration, these true tales would not have been possible.

To my ever supportive husband, Nick, thank you for always allowing me to follow my dreams.

To all the lovies on their own adventures – enjoy the ride!

First edition
https://www.facebook.com/authoramyvarcoe

Book design and illustrations by © 2018 Hanna Piepel Design Studio
www.hannapiepel.com

LOVEY
ADVENTURES

warm and **cozy**.

best friends for life.

Snuggle buddies. Stuffies or lovies,
all the same when you are scared,
tired or hurt —

our lovies are right by our side.
Ever wondered where they go and who
they meet? True tales of our lovies.

PUPPY

Laundry Adventure

One day at school, Puppy, Evan's lovey, heard a loud noise from the ceiling. Miss Annie, Evan's teacher, picked up the kiddos and their lovies, put them all in one crib and rushed them outside. Puppy heard Miss Annie say they were having a fire drill! In all the chaos Puppy got separated from Evan.

School was done for the day, Miss Annie was cleaning up and didn't see Puppy snuggled in the sheets and into the laundry bag he went.

Puppy wasn't sure where he was going, but he knew it wasn't home with Evan.

Mom and Dad looked and looked but could not find Puppy. It was almost Evan's bedtime. What were they going to do?

Mom tried green blankie, but Evan didn't want green blankie.

Evan started to cry. Mom tried Mr. Penguin, Dolly the Dolphin, Buster Bunny, but nothing was working. After crying for a long time, Evan FINALLY fell asleep...without Puppy.

Back at school...Puppy had been splished and splashed. Rubbed and dubbed.

When he opened his eyes he saw he was in the laundry room. Miss Annie realized she had put him in with the sheets. Out of the lost and found Puppy went and back to Evan's cubby. He couldn't wait to tell Evan all about his adventure smelling so clean!

LUMPY

Marathon Adventure

Lumpy was Mallory's Elephant.

Lumpy was on a road trip with her family to watch Mallory's mom run in a really long race called a marathon. After running 26.2 miles everyone was ready to go home.

Mallory's big brother Dylan had to go potty so badly and was in such a rush, he knocked Lumpy out of the car at a gas station parking lot on the way home.

Everyone was so tired that no one noticed Lumpy was missing until they got ALL the way back to home.

Luckily, the nice man working at the gas station saw Lumpy lying in the parking lot and didn't want anyone to run over her. He knew someone was missing Lumpy and would be back for her.

TO LUMPY

450 MILES TO SERVICES

Mallory's mom had checked every nook and cranny of the car, the suitcases and even her stinky running shoes. Just then she remembered stopping for gas. On the map she found the gas station and drove 450 miles back to get Lumpy.

Mallory had no idea what her mom did, but was
so happy to have Lumpy back by her side.

Mr. bear
Gone Missing Adventure

Mr. Bear was missing!

Kohen had not been able to sleep for a week. His mom had looked everywhere, used her magical mom powers, but Mr. Bear was NOWHERE to be found.

She had to find Mr. Bear! But where would she ever find another Mr. Bear?! She searched high and low, from California to Tupelo. Finally...

Two days later, the "new" Mr. Bear arrived at their house in a brown box.

Kohen's mom quickly started spilling juice on the "new" Mr. Bear and crushing crackers all over him. She even put toothpaste on his eye! (Just where Kohen had spilled it before.)

When Kohen got home from school he beamed with joy!
Mr. Bear was back with Kohen. Wink wink.

Bunny Bear had been sitting on a shelf at Grandma's house for
a long time, without a best friend. Bunny Bear always wanted
a best friend to explore and go on exciting adventures with him.
He liked hanging out with Blue Monkey, Wyatt's lovey, when he
came to play, but it just wasn't the same.

He wondered when he would get a best friend like Blue Monkey
and Wyatt.

Wyatt got a new baby sister, Eleanor, who was getting into
everything and taking all of his toys, including Blue Monkey.

Wyatt had an idea and showed Eleanor Bunny Bear. She loved
him and quickly became inseparable...and Blue Monkey was
safe with Wyatt. Eleanor and Bunny Bear went on adventures
everywhere together.

Both loved to eat scrambled eggs with a ketchup happy face on them for breakfast.

Both loved to have their toes stick out the bottom of the bed at nap time.

Both loved to ride in the grocery cart while snacking on a banana.

One day, Bunny Bear vanished. The search party went out, but Bunny Bear was nowhere to be found.

After giving up hope, Eleanor's mom was cleaning the toy room when she saw Bunny Bear's foot under the tent in the corner... Hank the dog's favorite spot to hide his toys.

Kitty Cat
Sleepover Adventure

One day Lucy's dad forgot to pick Kitty Cat up from school. Everyone at Lucy's school knew Kitty Cat always went home with Lucy at the end of each day.

Claire's mom noticed Kitty Cat was still there even though Lucy was already gone. Claire's mom took Kitty Cat home because she knew Lucy would be worried about Kitty Cat being all alone at school.

Kitty Cat loved every minute of her first sleepover at Claire's house.

She met new lovies, ate popcorn with candy mixed in and used flashlights to make hand puppets on the wall.

When Lucy came to school the next morning, Kitty Cat was safely in her cubby. Lucy squealed with joy. Kitty Cat had so much fun she couldn't wait to have another sleepover, this time with Lucy.

dougie GiRaffe
Hospital Adventure

Weston has to go to the children's hospital to get checked out to make sure he is healthy and able to run really fast. Every time he goes in he gets a wristband with his name and birthday on it, and so does Dougie.

Dougie has his own medical chart with his height, weight and allergies and of course his favorite food — bubble gum!

Dougie and Weston go through the cat scan, every time Dougie starts meowing and Weston reminds him it really isn't a cat doing the scan.

When it is time to get blood drawn, they count down from 5 and together they yell boom-shock-a-la-la!

No matter how sick Weston can get he can always count on Dougie being right by his side.

Through all the tears and snotty noses rubbed on your lovies, they will always have a special place in our HEARTS.

Now off for more

ADVENTURES.

BUNNY BEAR

LUMPY

MR. BEAR

KITTY CAT

Submit your lovey
photos and stories to
loveyadventures@gmail.com
to be featured in a special
online edition at
www.loveyadventures.com

Place your lovey photo
or drawing here!

DOUGIE GIRAFFE

PUPPY

BLUE MONKEY

PUPPY
Love established 2009
Owner: Evan, age 9

LUMPY
Love established 2010
Owner: Mallory, age 7

MR. BEAR
Love established 2009
Owner: Kohen, age 9

BUNNY BEAR
Love established 2014
Owner: Ellie, age 3

KITTY CAT
Love established 2010
Owner: Faye, age 8

BLUE MONKEY
Love established 2011
Owner: Wyatt, age 6

DOUGIE GIRAFFE
Love established 2012
Owner: Weston, age 5

Made in the USA
Lexington, KY
20 December 2018